"Bob Bliss is providing a significant service to the worlds of business and education by providing his readers an in-depth, first-hand account of what it takes to be an effective leader and manager. Bob has been just that – he's applied his practical hands-on, down-to-earth rules of the road in a wide variety of challenging situations – and achieved great results in each. If you want to walk in the shoes of a gentleman who has been a highly successful businessman, a first-class entrepreneur, and a very innovative educator, walk in Bob's. He's tops!"

Dr. Charles Stebbins
Brigadier General, USAF (retired)

"With this book Bob Bliss has given us the gift of years of business and educational insights learned through actual experience. The book concisely converges the science and theory of good business practice into an easily digestible set of pragmatic applications. If you are looking for a fresh perspective on leadership that illustrates good judgment time and time again, look no further".

B. Keith Fulton
President
Verizon West Virginia

"Bob Bliss has the uncanny ability to be able to see the forest and the trees. He does what is necessary to assure the survival of a company by combining focus on overall vision with implementation of effective day-to-day strategies. By aligning people with their skills and clearly defining expectations he gets the best out of employees while assuring the operational and financial integrity of the business".

Dr. David A. Clayman, Ph.D.
CEO/President, Clayman & Associates, LLC

Are You the Captain of the Love Boat or the Titanic?

How to Manage and Succeed in Time of Turmoil and Change

Practical Management for Business and Higher Education

Robert L. Bliss, BA, MA, LittD

authorHOUSE®

AuthorHouse™
1663 Liberty Drive
Bloomington, IN 47403
www.authorhouse.com
Phone: 1-800-839-8640

First published by AuthorHouse 4/23/2009

ISBN: 978-1-4389-7959-5 (sc)

Library of Congress Control Number: 2009903845

Printed in the United States of America
Bloomington, Indiana

This book is printed on acid-free paper.

Contents

Preface
Why Another Book?

When discussing the possibility of writing this book, the first question that came to my mind was, "Why another book on management?" There must be thousands of such books languishing on shelves everywhere. In my own experience, I have probably read fifty or sixty such books and have gained a little insight from most. However, the majority takes a somewhat professorial approach—they are teaching tools. In most cases that didn't hit my "hot button." In the course of my career, I have seen too many college and university instructors teaching strictly from a book, without ever having owned or managed a company, or in some instances having never had to meet a payroll.

This book will take a totally different approach, totally nonscientific, non–research oriented. It is, rather, a book designed to show the systematic management growth of one individual as he progresses through a series of management positions: the problems encountered, the various management styles observed, and his resulting style based on four simple words. The words will not be shocking or surprising to anyone in business or higher education, but their importance will be more clearly understood.

Why another book on management? Because I was asked—and with so many already on the shelf, what's one more?

Acknowledgments

Dedicated to my wife, Susan, for her love, understanding, and encouragement. To my daughters, Karen, Nancy, and Judy, my gratitude for putting up with moving four times in their formative years without too much complaining.

Special thanks to Paul Helmick and Deb Copeland for their encouragement and valuable advice, and to Dr. Martha Rader for her excellent editing.

Thanks also to Keith Fulton, Dr. Charles Stebbins, and Dr. David Clayman, for their support and confidence.

Prologue

"Challenges can be stepping stones or stumbling blocks.
It's just a matter of how you view them."
Unknown

Everyone faces challenges in his or her lifetime. How challenges are handled is a combination of determination, self-confidence, and an individual's overall outlook on his or her circumstances. Challenges can range from minuscule, minor, just average, to the truly major, those involving life-altering possibilities.

Minor challenges are just that—minor. They're an irritant—nothing you can't deal with without becoming too upset or discouraged. Long lines at the grocery store, running out of gas, meeting deadlines—none of these are life threatening. And while they may be irritating, they can be easily handled. Major challenges are an entirely different matter. They can easily alter an individual's life. Overcoming grief, for example, is not easy. Nor is facing physical disabilities or overcoming financial disaster, losing your job and not being able to find another one—and finally the real danger of lapsing into depression with the physical and mental issues that it entails.

How life's challenges are handled varies from person to person. Everyone has his or her own way of dealing with them. Some are always optimistic—they will find a way to overcome adversity, minor or major. Others are pessimistic—they throw up their hands in complete defeat. The challenge overcomes them. Some lack the foresight or ability to seek solutions. If the wall stops you, can you go around it? Can you go over it? Can you go under it? There are always options.

Here's a story of how one man confronted his challenge. This would be considered a major challenge, and one that could have easily ended entirely opposite of the actual scenario that resulted.

"A diamond is a chunk of coal that made good under pressure."
Anonymous

Raised on a farm, the young boy was small for his age—in fact in later years his father would comment that he "thought he was raising a dwarf." The small stature wasn't in itself a major obstacle initially, but it did draw attention to him on many occasions. The attention created unwanted notice of yet another obstacle—a severe speech impediment. The young boy stuttered to the degree that he later described it as "making Porky Pig sound like an eloquent speaker." This impediment was an obstacle in his early years of school. He was quiet in class, not wanting to be called upon, content to do his work without notice and leave. His parents arranged meetings with speech therapists from the school, and he met weekly with them for several months. While consuming in time, the results were less than satisfactory, not providing the change in speech everyone desired. Nevertheless, they continued periodically throughout elementary school and ceased when he entered junior high school.

Unfortunately, classes in junior high were inclined to have students speaking more in class. This presented a huge obstacle, both mentally and physically. If he could arrive late for class, he would—thinking the teacher would subject him to some punishment in the back of the room where he wouldn't be called on. This worked occasionally, but when he was called upon, his speaking would evoke covered laughter, snickers, and many comments from the other students both during and after class adjourned. His small stature was still evident, and this added to the obstacles he faced in school.

In junior high he discovered an interest in music. He was introduced to the trombone and began taking lessons. By the time he was in the ninth grade, he was a member of the high school marching band as well as the school-sponsored dance band. The latter played at every school dance and several other school functions. The boy also discovered he liked to sing—and he wasn't bad. In fact, he became the lead singer for the dance band and relished the times he could sing in front of an audience at these functions. Singing was the one way he could speak without stuttering!

Continuing on to senior high, his activities centered around music—expanding his time to include playing in a small combo with four musician friends. They played at the local yacht club, country club, and various charitable events throughout the region. Music became his passion at this point; he looked forward eagerly for opportunities to perform either at school or at a paid function. Work in the classroom, however, wasn't much improved. Being called upon to speak was still tough—and fellow students, while now used to his impediment, continued to be amused at his speaking attempts. Adding to the feeling of inadequacy was his designation as the "shortest boy in the class" for about the fourth year in a row!

As his senior year approached, talk of college was rarely mentioned. His parents were insistent he should apply—but he hoped to make a career with the U.S. Postal Service, following in the footsteps of his father and grandfather. Plus at the Post Office, there wouldn't be too many occasions where public speaking would be required. But fate played what—at the time—seemed a cruel trick, but it ultimately became a changing point in his life. The local college, Adrian College, offered him a scholarship based on his high school grades and class rank. His father told him it was now certain he was going to college! Reluctantly, the boy agreed and sent his application in just two weeks before the beginning of classes. During the latter part of his senior year of high school and the start of college life, Mother Nature decided to spring into action, and he started to grow! Life began to look a bit better!

"In the middle of difficulty lies opportunity."
Albert Einstein

Facing college initially was daunting: new faces among the students, new instructors, new surroundings, and totally new academic programs. All of this with the freedom of deciding whether or not to attend class! Totally different from high school! The young man decided this was perhaps an opportunity to shed his prior image of being the "shortest kid in school," the one who couldn't speak in front of a group, and the one with newfound bravado up front but self-doubt in reality. During new-student orientation that fall, he was unsure which classes to register for. Some courses were mandatory, but there was room for one or two electives. Selecting a business major, he swallowed hard and for one elective signed up for a class entitled Introduction to Speech. This was a major step! He was certain at that point that he would never complete the course, but it was "crunch time"—time to see if he could face his handicap head on.

When classes began the following week, he wasn't particularly looking forward to his first speech class. It met twice a week, so he had a few days to imagine all kinds of horror stories about the first class. He couldn't really concentrate on the other classes, such was his anxiety about the speech class. But the fateful day arrived all too soon. With fifteen other students, he arrived on time, took his seat and, sweating under a hot fall morning, listened as the instructor outlined the goals for the class. When the instructor finished, he then told the class to stand up one at a time and give a two- to three-minute introduction and background of themselves. After listening to five students speak, the boy was called upon, and with shaking knees, he rose to talk. His two- to three-minute introduction probably took ten to fifteen minutes, accompanied by worried glances from his classmates and, as usual, a few smiles and snickers in the group. But he persevered and finished his talk, probably to the relief of the other students as well!

Following this first class, the instructor took him aside and inquired if he was truly serious about taking a speech class. Seeing this as yet another rejection, the boy bristled inwardly and emphatically responded that yes, he was truly serious. And thus began a somewhat miraculous journey that few expected to see.

"You see things that are and say, "Why?"
"But I dream of things that never were and say, "Why not?"
George Bernard Shaw

After the awkward first class, things began to happen. The boy developed confidence, and he continued to grow physically. Repetition in speaking provided reinforcement, and practice developed new habits. Practicing in front of a mirror became standard procedure daily. Regardless of the assignment, he would sing in front of a mirror and suddenly stop singing and speak the words of the song. Gradually the speech impediment became less pronounced; not eliminated, but less noticeable. The first semester went by quickly, and with it a passing grade in Introduction to Speech! With the first hurdle complete, the boy decided to pursue a minor in speech and signed up for Discussion and Debate, Radio Workshop, and Interpretive Speech, all higher-level speech courses.

As time went by and more speech classes were completed, his confidence grew to the point where he was running for office in student organizations and working part time in the college public relations office. The ultimate prize came during his senior year, when he was asked to be the public address announcer at college basketball and football games! What a change!

Was the impediment eliminated? No—not entirely. To this day certain words create a slight hesitancy for him, but the confidence gained made every word possible without embarrassment or concern. After graduation, the young man began a career that he never thought possible. He rose quickly in key positions in higher education at one college and two universities, managing to acquire his master's degree along the way. His alma mater thought so much of his accomplishments later that they presented him with an honorary doctorate degree. He even became a college president, and after many years in higher education, became the president and owner of two corporations, leading four hundred employees and managing businesses covering four states.

> *"The quality of a person's life is in direct proportion to*
> *their commitment to excellence, regardless of*
> *their chosen field of endeavor."*
> *Vince Lombardi*

I'm certain the story outlined above is not unique—there are undoubtedly many others who have gone through a similar situation. And there are many others with more severe handicaps than he encountered. How the impediments are dealt with varies widely, being highly dependent on the determination and drive of the individual. In this particular situation, if not for the perseverance of his father and mother, this boy would have been totally content to work for the U.S. Postal Service for the remainder of his career. But life takes different directions, and the combination of a push by his parents and a suddenly developed determination to improve changed his life and career. Without this combination he would have taken a totally different path and probably one without the fun, excitement, and reward he has known.

Who was the boy? This is my story—the story of Robert L. Bliss— perhaps one of the luckiest persons on the face of the earth. Have the events of my early years affected my life? Most definitely, but in a most positive way. They have provided me with determination, perseverance, and an always positive outlook on whatever opportunities are provided. The paths chosen have been instructional, exciting, diverse, and truly educational. Working with and being responsible for the management and leadership of a wide variety of individuals has been a thrill.

Enjoy the book!

Top Three Tips

- In life or business, don't let challenges defeat you.
- Carefully outline your options for action.
- Determination and ambition cannot be easily identified.

Introduction

"You'll never prove you're too good for a job
by not doing your best."
Ethel Merman

Over the years friends and colleagues have asked many times, "How in the world can you manage people in two very distinct and opposite fields like business and higher education?" To them, it's like oil and water—the two just don't go together. One is profit driven, the other is nonprofit. One is product oriented, the other is education oriented. College and university boards of trustees are normally dominated by business leaders, many of whom feel faculty members don't have a feel for the "real world." Faculty members sometimes feel trustees have no concept of how an institution of higher learning should be run. In the faculty mind, college isn't a business. Are they vastly different, oil and water? Early in my career, I probably would have concurred, but experience has shown that management of people really depends on factors that actually cross occupational boundaries. It hinges on four words and putting a workable definition to each. Recognizing this has enabled me to develop a management style that has proven highly successful over the past forty years—transcending both business and higher education—a combination that has shown to be not only beneficial but very rewarding. The following pages will chronicle a journey through management experiences—some good, some bad— but all educational.

Walk through any bookstore in the United States today, and you will find hundreds of titles available on management. There is management theory, crisis management, personnel management, and so forth. And budding entrepreneurs will without hesitation purchase several books because they want to learn from the experts—and they want to learn *now*. Young entrepreneurs are bright—but many are also impatient, being born and raised in a generation accustomed to immediate gratification. And some make the mistake of believing their management expertise will be found solely in books. In reality, most entrepreneurs begin a business or venture because of their intense interest in one area—possibly the Internet or a new product to be manufactured or a new service to be offered. Most, if not all, usually will have a solid background in their specialty area. However, most, if not all, will have little background in management, especially of people. When and if their venture matures, they find themselves suddenly being a manager, a leader, and they run up against a wall of knowledge that they find lacking.

While at Northern Michigan University in Marquette, I had a colleague who wanted to take up golf. He purchased every imaginable book on the subject—Jack Nicklaus, Arnold Palmer, Ben Hogan, Sam Snead, and probably many others. After several months of consuming this huge amount of data and advice, he purchased a new set of golf clubs, a golf bag, and new golfing attire and then asked me to join him for his first trip to an actual golf course. On the agreed-upon day, he walked confidently to the first tee, took out his driver—and hit the first six balls out of bounds. The next ones either went straight up or off to the right or left, and a few even managed to make it a few feet off the tee. To his credit, he finished the first hole, then put the putter in his bag and walked off the course. He never played another hole of golf in the four years we worked together. He couldn't believe or understand why he couldn't drive the ball straight down the fairway. Like some entrepreneurs, he wanted instant gratification after reading all the books. How could he possibly not be a good golfer! Unfortunately, golf—like business—can't be 100 percent learned from a book. Books are great for gaining insight and ideas and sometimes learning how not to do something, in addition to how to do it correctly. But each book, by itself, is not a strictly defined road map for success. It requires much more.

So, like golf, or as in any profession, there truly isn't one single way to learn about management. As stated earlier, it cannot be contained in one book. It's a process that certainly incorporates the information from books, as many as you can read; however, this information must be intertwined with experience, judgment, and an understanding of people. Experience takes time, and judgment and understanding are equally difficult with time pretty much dictating the learning scale.

Having stated this, the following pages will present yet another "how to" on management—but with a twist. The difference will be in the substance presented. It's not theory based, nor is it scientifically based. It is, rather, experienced based and laced with practical experience from forty years of working with people in a wide range of business endeavors and in higher education. It's told through a biography of one person, the trials and errors encountered and the lessons learned from interaction with some of the nation's top business leaders, a variety of college and university presidents, and small business entrepreneurs—not to mention the personal experience of serving as a corporate president and college president.

Top Three Tips

- Entrepreneurs are not always fully ready for management.

- Management books are good, but not the final answer.

- Experience is never ending.

Chapter One

When Trouble Arises

"Inflation is bringing us true democracy. For the first time in history, luxuries and necessities are selling for the same price."
Robert Orben

In 1859 Charles Dickens wrote *A Tale of Two Cities*, and the book began with the following well-known words: "It was the best of times, it was the worst of times." While many have difficulty remembering the actual book, these words are familiar with a high percentage of the population. Perhaps not as well known are the words that follow the initial statement. The quote continues saying, "it was an age of wisdom, it was an age of foolishness."

It's been over 150 years since Dickens penned those words, but they very well could be applicable today. In light of the current economic situation and the ensuing failure and restructuring of businesses across the nation, we are definitely experiencing the effects of Dickens's words. And the repercussions are not limited solely to business; the economic situation has an immediate and costly effect on institutions of higher education as well. These effects are not as well documented or reported, but they are very real and require management just as precise to prevent potentially severe financial damage to the institutions.

When we are experiencing "the best of times" some leaders of education and business may have a tendency to view the world with rosy optimism. They want to enjoy their positive progress and may fail to have a contingency plan in place for any unforeseen calamity. Then, when confronted with "the worst of times," they are faced with a situation totally unfamiliar and for which they are not prepared. No one enjoys downturns—whether in business or education—but they are inevitable; they will occur at some point in both areas eventually.

This is where seasoned leadership is required. A strong "captain" must be at the helm. An individual with foresight, compassion, intelligence, strong ethics, and the ability to generate positive leadership in negative situations. Sounds like someone with a big red *S* on his or her shirt!

In a time of change, whether due to economic conditions or changing technology, leaders must be prepared to take positive and immediate action. The captain of a ship must decide in a crisis situation the correct steps to bring the ship safely to port. Hesitation, the wrong decision, or errors in not planning sufficiently may have disastrous results—like hitting an iceberg!

The analogy of the Love Boat or the Titanic outlines each scenario. Neither captain can be viewed as the "perfect" captain. Merrill Stubing, captain of the Love Boat, always brought his ship safely home to port. But he was seldom actually seen performing the duties of a captain. His main source of information and problem solving consisted of friendships with a bartender, cruise director, purser, and doctor. Not exactly a committee made up to effectively run a modern-day cruise ship. Captain Stubing was a leader who, in the long run, wanted to be liked. He dispensed wisdom and always looked at the rosy picture— never dwelling on the negatives or even planning for them.

Edward J. Smith, captain of the Titanic, is a complete opposite. He was a fine captain, always running a "tight ship," and received several promotions for his effective management. While enjoying the confidence of the board of directors, he was not going to upset anyone when the designers of the Titanic began making changes in the ship's construction: Fewer lifeboats than required to accommodate the entire list of passengers ("the ship is unsinkable"). No lifeboat drills required for the crew (same reason). The so-called watertight doors stopped five feet from the above deck ("the water will never rise high enough to overflow one to another").

His failure in leadership continued when, being pressured by the owners to set a new trans-Atlantic speed record, he continued to cruise at top speed in known iceberg-infested waters.

We all know the story—the Titanic hit an iceberg and sank in less than two hours, taking over fifteen hundred passengers to their deaths. Captain Smith, in the aftermath of hitting the iceberg, took twenty minutes before issuing the order to send a distress signal. He further hesitated in ordering the lifeboats to be lowered. When the crew received the order, they didn't know how to follow it! Chaos was the result.

In looking at your business or institution, would you fall into either of these categories—Love Boat or Titanic? It's easy to let it happen. Complacency is a deadly attitude for a leader, and it sometimes sneaks up on all of us, unless we don't allow it to happen.

Learning how to handle the unexpected isn't easy. It isn't fun. But it is required, because regardless of how well your company or institution is currently running, there will be a bump in the road, something to require a change in direction, or at worst, decisions to be made quickly to avert a major financial disaster.

Top Three Tips

- Good times are inevitably followed by bad times.

- Leadership without a contingency plan leads to disaster.

- Handling the unexpected takes practice and preparation.

Chapter Two
How It All Began

"Do the hard jobs first. The easy jobs will take care of themselves."
Dale Carnegie

Anyone reviewing my résumé will be quick to judge "the guy can't hold a job!" In actuality, while I have held a wide variety of positions in business and education, each has contributed greatly to my overall education and management style. To say I have been a willing victim of telephone calls would be an understatement—for each time I was convinced I was in my dream position, a telephone call (much to the chagrin of my daughters) would arrive, and a new challenge would be presented. One of my many faults is that I have a relatively short attention span. Once a challenge has been met and the initial excitement of creativity has diminished, my tendency is to become a bit bored and lackadaisical. Not good for anyone. So the telephone calls usually arrived at a very opportune time in nearly all occasions.

Having a variety of positions offering the opportunity to experiment, innovate, and create was not only intellectually stimulating, but it also afforded the opportunity to observe and develop a management style that has proven to be highly successful. Working closely with some outstanding—and some not so outstanding—leaders in business and education played a significant role in the development of this style. In the words of the Clint Eastwood movie, I've seen "the good, the bad and the ugly" and have learned from each of them.

In each position the management style was somewhat dictated by the objectives of the organization, whether it was education or business. There were educational institutions where the leader was driven solely by the bottom line financially, not necessarily educationally; there were others who were just the opposite. To attain their goals, different management philosophies had to be adopted, and one would not necessarily work in the other situation, although some tried and ultimately failed. In either scenario, the management of faculty or employees would be vastly different.

Additionally, there is some validity to geographical management styles playing a role. Business or education leaders in some regions of the country tend to be identifiably different from their counterparts in another region. Southern regions tend to have senior administrators more readily accessible, in terms of employee contact and sharing information. Northern states are a bit more formal and have a tendency to sometimes epitomize the image of the ivory tower mentality of management. The far West, California in particular, is different from either of these. There you find a blend of extreme informality to ultimate formality, depending on your location within the state. Bear in mind, none of this is scientifically proven—just observations from forty years of experience!

Regardless of the location, regardless of the business or educational institution, regardless of the objectives being sought—the proper management of people will dictate the success or failure of the organization. In throwing a wide net over the subject, people will usually respond to the same stimuli, even if it's provided in a variety of management styles. Over the course of my career, there are four words

I have found vital in the successful management of people, regardless of the occupation. They are *people, communication, responsibility,* and *accountability.* My rationale and conviction for using these words may be understandable to some, but for others the following justification is offered.

People: Too often when enjoying success in their lives, business and education leaders have a tendency to look in the mirror and congratulate themselves as the sole reason for that success. Reality may eventually hit them, either from comments from others or from finally realizing it takes many people and many positive circumstances to achieve success. Granted, there are individuals with the vision, drive, determination, and intelligence to succeed way beyond their expectations, but rarely is it accomplished alone. In my graduate classes, the question I always ask of budding master of business administration (MBA) candidates: "What is the most important commodity in a business or educational institution?" Answers vary in business from "inventory," "sales," "product," to finally "people," This holds true in education as well. Answers vary from "curriculum" to "reputation" to "strong athletics"!

People are the lifeblood of any organization, and many books have been written about this. And the way employees are motivated, energized, recognized, and rewarded holds the keys to the degree of success or failure of virtually any organization. Employees will run through a wall for the leader who recognizes them for their talent, who uses this talent to the utmost, who rewards the results, and who treats everyone fairly. Leaders following this format are usually those who leave their ego at the door and rarely see themselves in the mirror as being the sole reason for their success.

Communication: This word should be a no-brainer for those seeking professional advancement, in either the business world or higher education. It continually amazes me to see e-mails, letters, and papers with poor grammar, bad spelling, and misused words—but it happens every day. Students tell me, "I used spell check"—and I tell them the word might be spelled correctly, but it's the wrong use of the word! Simple words like *to*, *too*, and *two*; *sight*, *cite*, and *site*; and many other examples are frequently misused. In my MBA programs, candidates are constantly reminded that if they are unable to accurately, clearly, and confidently convey their message in written form, their qualifications for leadership will be seriously questioned.

Then we have the lack of ability of some budding leaders to communicate their thoughts, ideas, and visions orally. The top two fears of most people (in no particular order) are flying and public speaking. Flying today is common, but there are many who still have not boarded an airplane. While there are also many who have not been called upon to speak publicly, it is a necessity for executives in business and education. Like writing skills, speaking skills have to be honed through practice and experience. Careers have been launched, and lost, due to speaking skills. As in writing, it is mandatory for success that a speaker be confident, clear, concise, and able to convey his or her full mastery of the subject of the talk. Some have expressed that it is not really necessary to write or speak like a professional, as long as the message is conveyed. These are the ones who rarely last long in a key management position. The good ones excel at both.

Responsibility: Every organization has individuals who seek more responsibility, and in most this is a positive trait to have. Assuming responsibility is adding to the learning curve, and multitasking responsibility accelerates the curve in most situations. When individuals inquire about more responsibility, there are many thoughts that pass through my mind. First, are they doing above average work in their current position? Are projects finished on time with little or no corrections required? Is the individual one people like to work with—is there respect for his or her accomplishments? Does the individual have the background for additional responsibility; has he or she proven to be dependable? Second, is the motive behind the request to improve, help the organization, or is it to promote himself or herself? Or is it both? Occasionally individuals seek more responsibility to enhance their résumé and in the process truly desire to help the organization improve. The danger is employees who are seeking additional duties merely to improve their image within the organization or to reach a position that will enable them to be in a position of power. And that leads to the final word of the four.

Accountability: While nearly everyone will, at one time or another, actively seek additional responsibility, regardless of the motivation, it is difficult to find the employee who will stand up to accountability. Recent events have shown there are few leaders in business or industry, or education, who will step up without hesitation and be accountable for their decisions. Too many times we find individuals who—when faced with a decision that will have far-reaching consequences for their organization—decide to form a committee to evaluate the situation and recommend a decision. Should leaders use as much information as possible from their employees? Absolutely, and they should include information from as many possible individuals available. However, after digesting and discussing the information, the ultimate decision must be made at the top and not by a committee. Leaders abdicate their role when the decision is announced as one made by a committee. A committee provides a convenient excuse when decisions are not popular or result in financial loss.

Of the four words in management, accountability is the most difficult to truly attain in an individual. The four are all intertwined, but they can be totally destroyed by a leader who runs from accountability when true leadership is required. Virtually anyone can lead when decisions are easy, and everything is running smoothly. True leaders must have accountability first and foremost in their management style.

How these four words became embedded in my management philosophy is best described in the following pages—a chronicle of receiving telephone calls at sometimes crucial points in my life, but always at a time when change was welcome. The learning experience through the variety of management philosophies observed was priceless.

Top Three Tips

- Today's leaders/entrepreneurs rarely remain long in the same position.

- Entrepreneurs usually have a short attention span outside of their area of expertise.

- Managers should remember four key words: people, communication, responsibility, and accountability.

Chapter Three
A Crash Course in Crisis Management

"If the only tool you have is a hammer,
you tend to see every problem as a nail."
Abraham Maslow

The first official position I had in higher education was at Adrian College in Michigan. With just a couple of months to go before I graduated from Adrian, I was prepared to go to work for an advertising company in Detroit. About that time, the president of the college asked me to come to his office. It was a shock and a thrill when he asked if I would be interested in remaining at the college after graduation as assistant to the president. Being young and naive, I immediately accepted the offer—and my first true lesson in management was about to begin. (Truth be known, the title sounded better than "ad man.")

My venture into higher education administration began the Monday after graduation. During my initial talk that day with the president, he informed me the board of trustees had given him one academic year to show a positive turn for the college, or the board would be forced to close the doors. Needless to say my "contract" was possibly limited to a very brief nine months. But this president had a vision for the institution—one that few fully understood or believed. He saw survival—and he saw an institution with enormous potential.

To fulfill his vision, he very wisely surrounded himself with a few truly outstanding individuals in key positions. He had a Development director who was dynamic. He had a Public Relations/Admissions director who was innovative and imaginative. Veteran financial officers were in place, and the president was free to devote more time to fund-raising, alumni meetings, corporate meetings, and convincing board members of the viability of his vision.

At the time, his management style was somewhat dictatorial in nature—it was his way or no way—but difficult times demanded a strong hand. Faculty members weren't always happy with their lack of involvement, but they were greatly pleased when they were awarded their first pay increase in nearly three years. Watching and working closely with the president provided tremendous insight into the workings of a very dedicated individual. He was insightful in hiring the right people—way before hiring the "right person in the right seat of the bus" became popular. He was decisive and, right or wrong, continued to move forward to make the institution financially and educationally viable.

Was he accountable? Absolutely—in every sense of the word and without apologies. Mistakes would be acknowledged, but never apologized for—they were learning steps. Was he a good communicator? Definitely—public speaking was his strength, and being able to convey his goals to a wide audience was a positive. Did he communicate with all of his constituents, that is, faculty? Perhaps not as often or effectively as he could have, but dramatic change sometimes dictates limited communication.

While my title officially was "assistant to the president," the actual duties went far beyond the title. I was assigned the task of creating the first official Alumni Relations Office, including initiating three alumni clubs in surrounding states. Student housing and employment, on-campus and off-campus, were on my résumé. Assisting in admissions was added; in that first year I called on over two hundred high schools in a three-state area. Working with the public relations director, I was involved in writing, editing, and publishing a monthly alumni magazine. In my "spare time," I announced at all football and basketball games! Quite a switch for someone who, just a few years earlier, avoiding speaking on the telephone. All of these duties involved working with a variety of educators, business people, and students, and obtaining cooperation with each.

One year later, Adrian College remained open, and it is a strong and viable private college today. The president who turned the college around remained in that office many years, and some say, too many. His management style was perfect for the hard times, but as the college grew in students and faculty, his style became increasingly less effective. It was a time of change in higher education, and dictatorial management was becoming the dinosaur technique, and he began to have a very difficult tenure. Lesson learned? Perhaps management styles should change as the situation changes. Putting my toe into higher education for this year was invaluable in my learning process.

Top Three Tips

- Always conduct thorough due diligence.
- Dictatorial management may not be all bad.
- Management styles should change with the situation.

Chapter Four
A Different Management—Military Style

"I like work: it fascinates me. I can sit and look at it for hours."
Jerome K. Jerome

Just prior to the conclusion of my first year of employment, the U.S. Army beckoned. Following commencement ceremonies at the college, I found myself on a bus headed for eight weeks of basic army training. I was one of 180 young men who departed from the induction center in Detroit, Michigan, for initial training at Fort Polk, Louisiana, followed by an additional eight weeks at Fort Chaffee, Arkansas. At our initial swearing in, we were informed that this particular group was scheduled for occupation duty in the Far East, probably in Korea. We should notify our families that evening in case we were unable to have leave time before leaving the United States.

Management in the military is different from business or higher education—but it is management for that particular organization—and it works! The U.S. military is not a democratic model of management, and leaders are trained to inspire teamwork and trust in the team. It's yet another type of "situational leadership." It doesn't seek continual input of ideas, suggestions, or discussion on the mission or objective. It does strive to provide unquestioning obedience to authority. For some, their first exposure to this type of leadership can be frustrating and discouraging, yet it is necessary in the framework of the organization. When orders are given, immediate response is required—no committees, no focus groups, and no voting.

After sixteen weeks of training, 179 of my fellow trainees departed for the Far East for duty either in Vietnam or Korea—and for reasons yet undetermined, I was assigned to the Headquarters Division of the North American Air Defense Command (NORAD) in Colorado Springs, Colorado. Prior to leaving Fort Chaffee, Arkansas, the commander of my training group called me to his office. He indicated he "didn't know who the heck I knew, but I was being assigned to NORAD Headquarters." I replied that I didn't know anyone, but was very pleased to be going to Colorado! I have no idea why this occurred and have never questioned it!

While still in the army, the management at NORAD was totally different from the preceding sixteen weeks! I reported to a one-star army general and was the only army personnel under his command of thirty-plus officers—the others being U.S. Air Force personnel. My general was unique in the military. He sought opinions; he consulted his colleagues and, while rank was always important, rarely used his position as one of power. The remaining twenty months of my military service were spent at NORAD. I counted my military experience as yet another step in the learning curve of management, where teamwork, responsibility, and accountability were valued. The air force officers were varied in duties, but all were pilots. They displayed a variety of management styles in managing the enlisted personnel under them. Unlike my general, some relished their rank and made certain they were treated accordingly. Others sought a cooperative style, seeking input when and where needed. In my assignment, it was required that I wear civilian clothes, so rank was never a problem, and my relationship with all the officers was professional and cordial. The fact that I reported directly to the general didn't hurt!

Returning to Adrian College from the military was yet another experience. In two years many things change—personnel, objectives, and unfortunately, leadership. I spent another two years at Adrian College and, while the experience was vastly different from my initial year there, the time spent was productive. I was growing in maturity and seeing firsthand how quickly management styles can change, and not always for the better. My trust and faith in one individual's management was wavering, and the next few months were productive in learning more about higher education and, perhaps just as much, about the uncertainty of management stability.

Initially the president's management style (dictatorial) was required: the college was rapidly going into bankruptcy, and immediate change was necessary. However, once stability was achieved, his style quickly became an irritant, especially to faculty. The result was the emergence of four unions on a campus of less than one thousand students. While acknowledged as the savior of the institution, the president was also criticized for his failure to adapt to a new management environment. The savior definition probably added to the ego factor—never learning to leave it at the door.

> *Management Lesson: Effective management usually will fall under the guise of situational management. Conditions change, circumstances change, and when this occurs, management styles will usually change. In some cases this may not occur; however, good, effective leaders must be able to adapt to the personnel and the situation surrounding them. Failure to do so will result in declining faith in the business or educational leadership.*

Top Three Tips

- Nondemocratic management can work.

- Leaders in this style can still use the four key words effectively.

- Things are never the same the second time.

Chapter Five

Management—Statewide Level

"Experience is simply the name we give our mistakes."
Oscar Wilde

Slightly more than two years after returning to Adrian College, I received a call from Michigan State University (MSU). The director of admissions and scholarships was looking for an associate director and asked if I would be interested in the position. With some trepidation about the move to a major university of forty thousand–plus students, I responded positively, and within a few days, found myself being interviewed by the entire admissions and scholarships professional staff as well as the vice president for special projects to whom the director of admissions reported. Meeting the vice president was yet another revelation in management. He was viewed with anxiety by the staff, who were nearly always fearful of meeting with him face to face. He was brilliant, constantly bringing new programs, new ideas, and innovation to the Admissions program, but he was intense in his determination for excellence and his intolerance for less than perfection in performance.

Prior to meeting him, nearly all of the current staff members asked, "Have you met Mr. X yet?" And all of the questions were asked with a feeling of impending doom! When I actually met Mr. X, I found him to be inquisitive, friendly and—not surprisingly—very direct in questioning and in pursuing details when answers were provided. Having listened to his staff's concerns, I decided to use his tactic of direct questioning and pursuing details! To my relief, he responded positively, and I was hired before leaving his office

So what was learned? I found Mr. X to be a good manager—not great, but good. He liked to manage his staff by what may be termed "semi-intimidation." He enjoyed having the staff somewhat fearful of him, yet at the same time tended to reward and share confidences with those who didn't feel intimidated. During my two years at Michigan State, Mr. X and I became not only colleagues but good friends. I found later that I was the only one (ever) on the staff to invite Mr. X and his wife to my home for dinner. Most of the staff was hesitant to even invite him to their office.

Mr. X remained a good friend for many years. We corresponded frequently after we parted company professionally. To me, he was an example of management by intimidation but complemented with the ability to accommodate those willing to present their own views in a confident manner. The most successful among the Admissions and Scholarship staff were those who had that ability.

During my tenure at MSU, my speaking skills were greatly enhanced as well. In addition to speaking before hundreds of high school students and their parents, the Admissions staff participated in a unique scholarship program. We gave commencement addresses all over the state of Michigan, with our honorariums devoted to academic scholarships for Michigan students. In my two years, I presented commencement addresses at many high schools, with graduating classes ranging in size from ten to two thousand. Each was unique and required sometimes very unique people skills. Speaking to a class of ten was more personal and informal, and the talk could be adapted to meet the expectations of the audience. Speaking to an audience of two thousand, in an outdoor football field, required different skills entirely. It was more formal, less individualized, and perhaps requiring a bit more preparation!

> *Management Lesson: Adaptability in everyday contacts is a must. Whether a small group or large, the audience has expectations. Advance preparation will usually pinpoint the expectations, and without that preparation, an excellent speech can deteriorate into a disaster rather quickly. Know your audience—know the people to whom you are speaking. Know your subject matter.*

> *Management Lesson: My now former employer was angry and felt betrayed by my departure. Despite the obvious professional advancement, he began to view me as an adversary for the remaining days of my tenure on campus. To me, it's a compliment to your management when employees are sought out by others. Perhaps you hired very well! Give them your best wishes and congratulations—you may want them back some day.*

Top Three Tips

- Take advantage of opportunities.
- Don't become a victim of intimidation.
- Never burn bridges—you never know when you may meet again.

Chapter Six
Management with Ultrastrong Accountability

"Only those who want everything done for them are bored."
Billy Graham

Michigan State University was an excellent academic institution, and my learning curve was rising as responsibilities increased. However, once again, the telephone rang. It was the president of Northern Michigan University (NMU), located in Marquette. He was going to be in East Lansing the following week and asked if we could have lunch. I learned a long time ago, when a college or university president invites you for lunch or dinner, it's usually wise to accept—if for no other reason than curiosity.

Meeting Dr. Edgar Harden for lunch the following week proved to be one of the smartest and most educational meetings in my life to that date. Dr. Harden had been president of NMU for eleven years and said he needed a complete revamping of the Admissions and Financial Aid office at the university. The enrollment was stagnant at four thousand students, faculty morale concerning student quality was extremely low, and in reality, the entering students were not of the caliber he desired. Faculty described the university as "the school you went to after flunking out somewhere else"—or—"if you couldn't gain admissions somewhere else, apply to NMU." After I made a trip to the campus, I found the challenge he presented was too enticing to refuse, and the faculty description was verified. In brief, he indicated he wanted a significant increase in enrollment, an increase in student quality, and the creation of a formal Admissions and Financial Aid office. I would be a one-person operation—unheard of at that time! Even the smallest college in Michigan had an admissions staff of three to five professionals—and I was taking over a university admissions office where I was the only employee! It was at NMU where I became very aware of the word *accountability* in the full meaning of the word. I reported only to Dr. Harden and was given free rein to establish admissions guidelines and revamp (create?) a new department that included the admissions, financial aid, and registrar's offices. Dr. Harden, in his hopeful wisdom for this new employee, relied solely on my judgment. But—also in his wisdom—he expected results without excuses and professionalism beyond reproach.

Rapid and careful decision making became necessary early in my tenure at NMU. While I was reading the paper one Sunday, a startling headline jumped out at me. It read, "Freshman student convicted for killing father. Still planning to enroll at NMU." The actual murder had taken place some six months previously, but the trial had just been completed. The article went on to state the student had been accepted for admission to the university for the coming fall semester. The article stated further that due to the circumstances of the case, the student was convicted on a lesser crime and placed on probation so he could attend NMU.

My first stop was my office to check the student's file. The academic record indicated a strong 3.00 grade point average, good scores on the SAT, and excellent recommendations from the high school guidance counselor. The next day I contacted the counselor by phone, and when asked why this situation wasn't revealed with the application, either by letter or telephone, she "didn't want to hurt their chance for admission." Within hours telephone calls were being received at in my office from anxious parents about their son or daughter enrolling with a "convicted murderer." Rumors were springing up faster than the facts could be explained. By the end of the week, a meeting was arranged in Detroit, Michigan, with the student involved, the mother, and their lawyer. Following lengthy discussions, a joint statement was issued indicating "the student's admission was being reversed based on false information on the application for admission." Once again, rumors developed, and angry calls were received condemning the reversal. Behind-the-scenes arrangements were made for the student to enroll quietly at another state university under a different name to avoid the publicity and distraction.

This situation was stressful in many ways, but again, it was a learning experience. Things are not always as they appear, and first impressions can many times be wrong. In this entire scenario, Dr. Harden left the decision making in my hands—he expected good judgment, honesty, and integrity at all times. To me, that was the mark of an exceptional leader. Dr. Harden combined the best of all management textbooks. He was demanding, patient, understanding, and willing to listen, while in the end expecting positive results that could be measured, results that enabled the university to grow in a spectacular manner.

He departed the university after my third year, and his replacement didn't have the same management style. He wanted control over admissions and financial decisions in the president's office—and indicated that faculty members could admit any student in their academic area that they recommended—completely circumventing the admissions process, including grades, counselor recommendations, and test scores. The end result was a drop in morale among the admissions and financial aid staff. The change also raised many questions among high school guidance counselors throughout the state of Michigan. Talk about a quick switch in management styles!

One year later, the telephone rang once again. This time the call was from the National Merit Scholarship Corporation—the nation's largest scholarship-awarding firm in the country. The president offered me the position of director of College Programs nationwide. I had accomplished the goals at NMU that Dr. Harden had requested. Enrollment increased from four thousand students to eight thousand with a significant increase in student quality. The university's stature among guidance counselors in Michigan was higher than ever, and our admissions program was looked upon as one of the best in the state. While the new opportunity with National Merit was enticing—and accepted—my tenure at NMU has to be one with the highest points in learning about management of people. And going from one of the best to one not quite as highly regarded served me well as my education continued.

Top Three Tips

- Meet accountability head-on with confidence.
- Learn from leaders you respect.
- Accept as much responsibility as possible.

Chapter Seven

Management at the National Level

"You can't build a reputation on what you are going to do."
Henry Ford

The challenge at the National Merit Scholarship Corporation was one of organization at the national level. Since Michigan State University had begun actively recruiting Merit Scholars in 1962, a substantial number of other institutions had begun doing the same. The concern was a lack of central control of the programs and policing new programs to ensure they complied with the regulations of the Merit Corporation. This proved to be an invaluable management learning experience. The president was an intelligent man, with the ability to delegate responsibility and accountability to those he deemed able to meet his expectations. His vice president was one of the most intelligent individuals I have ever been blessed to work beside. She, too, delegated, but was perhaps a bit more firm in her expectations and definitely expected accountability.

While in this position, I traveled across the country meeting with college and university presidents from institutions of all sizes. Some presidents remain vividly in my mind because of their excellent management skills, both academically and financially. They were well thought of by faculty and staff alike and, not unexpectedly, several

27

moved rapidly up the ladder to institutions with larger enrollments and responsibilities. Obviously, there were others on the opposite end of the scale. To assist my recommendations on the campus and my assessment of the president, I developed a procedure that would provide maximum information on both areas in a relatively brief period of time. My usual routine when visiting a campus to meet with the president would be to arrive a day early. That day would be used to meet students in the student union for coffee and inquire about the institution, the faculty, the administration, and the college in general. This would be followed by inviting a few faculty members to have coffee with me— again, asking the same questions. Having three daughters, I began my conversations indicating I was looking for an institution for them and wanted information on this particular school. Students and faculty alike were usually very candid in their observations, especially for a free cup of coffee. At dinner that evening, I asked questions of the waitperson about the relationship between the city or town and the institution—what is their opinion? When the time arrived the next day to meet with the president and ask the same questions, it always amazed me the number of times the answers were poles apart. It told volumes about the management style and perception of the president. It was always a pleasure to meet the presidents who had high rankings among faculty, staff, students, and the town. They were the ones who were not only effective in their present position, but they were high on the radar screens of institutions where their colleagues weren't quite as effective in their management.

After three years working with colleges and universities, I was elected vice president of the corporation with responsibility for Sponsor Services. This involved a major switch in direction, as it required working with the Fortune 500 executives on their employee-child scholarship programs. While Northern Michigan University provided a good contrast in higher education management, working with the Fortune 500 executives was an opportunity to view management on a much different level. I had expected corporate executives, especially a Fortune 500 CEO/president, to be somewhat aloof, impatient, and serious minded. On a few occasions my expectations were right on target; however, in the majority of cases, just the opposite was true. The vast majority of executives I met were very gracious, patient, and interesting individuals—totally different from my expectations. In conversations with them, it was quickly apparent that "situational management" was the norm rather than the exception. While most had a professional background relating to their current position, quite a few were "generalists." They possessed the ability to work with a wide range of individuals, projects, and professions. They didn't have to be experts in just one specific area to be successful. This was perhaps the first time my eyes were opened to the fact that future (or hopeful) leaders shouldn't necessarily limit themselves in their ability to lead others. In most cases, having a broad range of management ability was more valuable than having expertise in just one area of specialization. Being able to motivate, inspire, and lead employees in a nearly foreign environment professionally was intriguing to me. I quickly learned through conversations that such an experience could prove to be an uphill battle for someone if their training and background in a particular organization was limited, or totally absent. Imagine the reaction of employees when a total stranger to the profession was named CEO/president! Immediate thoughts of total disaster came to mind—"What could our directors be thinking!" "This is going to be a short-lived presidency!" Every possible negative thought would be running rampant through the organization—talk about a tough leadership position. Little did I know at the time that I would one day be in that position.

As difficult as this appeared, these individuals impressed and inspired their employees. Not only were they placed in management and leadership positions where their expertise and abilities were immediately questioned, but they assumed the new opportunity with determination and confidence. These were the ones who had a noticeable impact on my management style. Without actually acknowledging it inwardly, the years spent working with the Fortune 500 executives were undoubtedly some of the most educational of my career. Working with executives from some of the top corporations in the United States provided an experience without parallel. Their varying management styles highlighted the importance of emphasizing those four words: *people, communication, responsibility, and accountability.* The impact they had would become clearly evident in the very near future. Had I not received another phone call I was convinced the National Merit Corporation would be my employer until retirement.

Top Three Tips

- Due diligence comes in many forms.
- Most successful leaders are the easiest with whom to work.
- The four key words are always used.

Chapter Eight
Crisis Management—Good and Bad

"Be nice to people on your way up because
you meet them on your way down."
Jimmy Durante

While I enjoyed the education and learning with the National Merit Corporation, and mainly my association with top national executives, the initial challenge wasn't quite as strong and began to diminish. Sponsor Services was becoming routine, and much of my business could be conducted rather quickly over the telephone because I had established personal relationships with the executives. This was definitely a plus for business, and personally it was gratifying to count a number of these executives as friends.

Finally, after seven years with the Merit Corporation I received a call from a head-hunting firm in Chicago. The caller indicated he represented a small college seeking a new president. Over lunch he detailed the situation. The college was nondenominational, had an enrollment of roughly nine hundred students, with the majority commuters, and was in severe financial difficulty. Students were leaving, faculty hadn't had a pay raise in three years, and the school was heavily in debt to many vendors in the state. In a final desperate effort, the board of trustees had offered the college to the state free of charge. The state turned down the offer, primarily due to the extreme indebtedness. It was then decided to hire another president. Before contacting me, the college had actually hired two other presidents, but before arriving on campus, both had changed their minds and refused the offer. The college was Morris Harvey College (now the University of Charleston) in Charleston, West Virginia.

After two visits to the campus and numerous meetings with trustees, faculty, students, alumni, and townspeople, an offer was made and accepted. Within two months, I arrived on a beautiful campus situated on the Kanawha River directly across from the West Virginia state capitol. Many colleagues questioned my sanity in leaving a top position for one with questionable chances for survival, and one where a candidate from another state would undoubtedly meet opposition. In retrospect, it is clear my background in higher education almost always placed me in a position where change was required. This fell into that category, but the change required was immense in comparison with previous positions.

Shortly after arriving on campus and meeting with faculty, students, and staff, three members of the executive committee of the board came to my office. They informed me that fund-raising was not to be my immediate concern. They—the board—would continue to handle that, and my efforts should be focused on the morale of the faculty, students, and alumni. This was a surprise, as one of my functions at National Merit was fund-raising, and the contacts I had established with national foundations were very strong. It was stranger still that in our initial talks it was indicated that fund-raising would be high on the to-do list in light of the deficit situation of the college. I quickly discovered that while, as president, I reported to the board of trustees, there was a segment of the board that was used to—and desired to continue—making day-to-day decisions on the operation of the college. This became yet another lesson in management, a lesson quickly learned by some, slowly or never learned by others.

The primary function of a collegiate board of trustees is to hire a competent president and to *not* become involved in the daily operation of the institution. This became decision time when, after nearly a year, the fund-raising efforts were less than successful. I decided at that point to call ten of my former foundation contacts, inquiring if they would be interested in spending a couple of days on our campus (at their expense). Obvious to all of them, my reason was to solicit some form of financial assistance from their foundations. All ten accepted, and they were hosted on campus for two days, learning the history, the projected future, and the positives and the negatives of the college. Upon departure, all indicated they would welcome a proposal from the institution. No guarantee, but they would give serious consideration to any proposal received.

The following Monday morning the board chairman came to my office and wanted to know who the people were that we hosted on campus. It was explained why, and what we hoped to achieve—the possibility of receiving as much as $10 million in badly needed funding. It was shocking, to say the least, when he responded that the board didn't want any outside money coming to the college. If that occurred, the donating organization would "want to run the institution," and that was the board's function only. The next few months were tense. While the situation was far from perfect, there were still lessons to be learned which, again, would prove valuable in the future. Sometimes presidents have lengthy tenures, while for others the stay is relatively brief. Is one better than the other? Possibly, but usually the "educational marriage" turns out to be a bad fit when the tenure is short. In my situation it was a bad fit—and perhaps the only time in my career where I failed to perform sufficient due diligence.

Management Lesson: There can never be too much due diligence, whether visiting a college, university, or business for a day or for employment. Patience is a virtue, and slow and easy in most instances results in better results in the long run.

(Before continuing, it must be noted that the University of Charleston today is not only a vastly different institution, but is listed as one of the top fifteen private institutions in the South. It has leadership—it has vision—and is continually looked upon as a model for innovation in higher education.)

As if on schedule, another telephone call was received—one that would take me in a totally different career path and one that would prove to be yet another learning challenge.

Top Three Tips

- Always be prepared for the next opportunity.
- Be positive in changing to a new position.
- Hold to the principles that have proven successful.

Chapter Nine

Crisis Management in Business

"I do not pray for a lighter load, but for a stronger back."
Phillips Brooks

A member of the board of trustees who didn't agree with the executive committee contacted me via a telephone call and asked if I was "married to higher education." When I responded definitely not, he invited me to join him for a weekend in the Bahamas to discuss a career change. Arriving on Andros Island, he indicated he had a family-owned company, doing very well—that he was primarily a salesman, but was looking for someone to serve as vice president to work on personnel and management issues. After two days of discussion (and sun), I accepted the position—and a major management eye-opener awaited me.

His company was a distributor for a major diesel engine and transmission manufacturer with seven locations in four states. They had approximately three hundred employees. The company was owned jointly by the president and his two sisters. Several things happened rather rapidly in the first months of employment. First, I discovered there was resentment on the part of some employees to the "new hire" taking a vice president's position. (Remember the earlier discussion on individuals moving into a management position without prior experience in that field?) And second, the company purchased a new airplane for roughly $1.5 million, to be used for travel between the branches and entertaining customers on long weekends in the Bahamas. This purchase was made because the company was "making so much money." The following months were spent reviewing the management operations of each branch location, from personnel utilization to marketing, financial stability, and customer relations. It wasn't long after that when I discovered that the company—rather than being highly profitable—was, in fact, rapidly losing money and heading to bankruptcy. Sales were actually increasing 25 percent annually—but expenses were increasing at 50 percent. The president was an excellent salesman; however, he was overlooking the expense part of the ledger. It didn't take long before banking officials and the engine/transmission manufacturer were concerned enough to schedule a meeting with the owners. At the conclusion of the meeting, a new president/general manager had been named—me. Still lacking significant knowledge of the product, I had to rely on identifying and working with qualified *people, communicating* goals, seeking those capable of more *responsibility,* and holding them *accountable.*

Within the first month, several steps were taken to reverse the financial trend. Each step was undertaken after discussion with key management personnel—some of whom were those opposed to my appointment. Communication was the key, as well as keeping everyone informed on the ultimate goal—to make the company financially solvent in the short term, and financially strong for the long term.

Some of the more difficult decisions were the following:

- Reassignment of some branch managers. Many had been appointed because they were well liked as mechanics—but had little or no management training. Expectations were outlined, and the current managers were afforded the opportunity to return to work as mechanics. Several elected to do so. Those replaced were returned to mechanic status, and all were thankful for the change. New managers were appointed, where required, with the understanding they would be totally responsible for the operation of their branch: hiring, termination, profitability, and budgeting. Training was initiated for each manager.

- Sale of the new company airplane. The operational cost (hangar, pilot, and hourly cost) was prohibitive in light of the financial situation.

- Elimination/sale of company automobiles. I established a monthly car allowance for sales staff—nothing for company executives and managers.

- Revamp of the fringe benefit program for all employees.

- Development of incentive bonus programs at all levels.

These changes, along with several others, represented crisis management at its best. Changes had to be made quickly, efficiently, and profitably while maintaining clear and concise communication with all employees.

Employees fear change even when expected. When change occurs unexpectedly, it is doubly difficult and unsettling unless you have total communication.

Perhaps the most effective tactic was the one most highly questioned. All of the hourly employees had complained for some time about wages and fringe benefits—both, in their opinion, were too low. Realizing the impossibility of increasing either, I invited the wives of our mechanics to join me for lunch in the best restaurant in their respective city or town. This required meetings in seven locations in four states. The response was overwhelming, and while my peers questioned my sanity for taking this route, to me it made sense to speak with them about finances. At each luncheon I was the only representative of management and conducted what amounted to a "fireside chat" with the wives. Using a flipchart, I showed them the income and expenses of the company, along with copies of the previous month's financial statements. Line item expenses were compared to those of a typical household. By the end of the luncheon (about two to three hours), all questions had been answered. To my relief, the wives became my strongest supporters in my quest to make the company profitable again.

To list all of the events taking place would require volumes of text. The employees at this stage were experiencing every possible emotion—fear, anxiety, frustration, and even excitement. It was gratifying to see the majority coming on board with the changes that were rapidly happening and bringing even better ideas for change to the new management team.

Within the first year, the company had transitioned from an estimated loss of $850,000 to a profit of $1.2 million. The second year, the profit was even better. At this point, I made the decision to purchase the company. With the cooperation of the original lending bank, a leveraged buyout was arranged, and a loan was established.

"The way I see it, if you want the rainbow,
you gotta put up with the rain."
Dolly Parton

Leaders are always challenged. The challenge can come in a variety of ways and is always intriguing to the true entrepreneur. The test is how the challenge is approached—and how it is conveyed to other managers and employees. Roughly six months after purchasing the company (based on a sizeable personal loan at 1 percent over prime), it was a substantial shock when the prime rate rose to 22 percent—and we were then required to pay 23 percent interest on the bank loan. This was *crisis management* in the true sense of the phrase. Coping with this threat required innovation, creativity, patience, and confidence. There are several ways of dealing with crisis situations. Some crises are relatively minor, but are viewed as crises because everything had been going smoothly and even a small bump in the process creates a certain amount of anxiety. A minor crisis could be the loss of a key department manager with no immediate replacement in sight. It could also be an unexpected drop in sales that is worse than anticipated. The crisis faced by my newly acquired company at this time was a major crisis—the potential loss of the company due to national economic conditions over which we had no control.

For any leader, this is perhaps the ultimate test of leadership, ingenuity, and perseverance. Decisions made at this point would determine the viability of the company. Immediate action was required to stem the impending flow of red ink. With a seven-figure note at the bank, the 23 percent interest rate was draining cash flow more rapidly than sales to replace it. Long hours and hard decisions were the norm, as employee productivity was reevaluated, every line item expense was subject to intense scrutiny, fringe benefits were reviewed, floor plan inventory was reduced, vehicles were parked, and corporate salaries were reduced. Raises for all employees were frozen. Even with these actions, the viability of the company was in real danger of bankruptcy. And then, another opportunity presented itself. However, this presented yet another crisis decision to be addressed. Company advisers (accountants and lawyers) were not enthusiastic about a possible new venture at this juncture; in fact, they questioned my judgment and sanity when it was initially discussed.

Top Three Tips

- Confidence is vital when undertaking a totally new profession.

- Crisis management can be reduced to individual management.

- Accountability is a mandatory strength.

Chapter Ten
Creating a Totally New Company

"Sometimes in the winds of change we find our true direction."
Anonymous

The new idea was born during a period of uncertainty and pressure. It's often been said that opportunities become apparent in time of trouble and turmoil. While we were struggling with falling revenues of the diesel engine company, one part of the company was fairly profitable, but limited in actual production.

One of our product lines was a line of remanufactured diesel engine parts. This was a line of rebuilt diesel engine parts that were remanufactured to new specifications and sold for approximately 80 percent of a new part. It was a fine line of products—but again, we weren't really selling that much. In assessing the locations and facilities we had under the diesel company, there was one that didn't quite fit the mold of the others. An Ohio facility had been obtained by the original owners to be used as a central parts distribution building. It was anticipated to have electronic parts-picking, automated carts, and to be nearly 100 percent computer operated. It never reached this potential and was now being used partially for parts, but with a high volume of unused floor space. The building was roughly 125,000 square feet in total.

With the diesel engine company floundering financially—primarily with the heavy bank debt—I decided to roll the dice and spin off the Ohio location into a totally new company. It was incorporated as "Bliss Enterprises, Inc." With no customers, no trained employees, but with a strong belief in our vision for what might be, we entered the remanufacturing business in a big way.

Initially we set up a production line to remanufacture small engine components, injectors, rocker arms, and so forth that could be easily handled and quickly manufactured. We trademarked our brand name, Rebex, designed boxes for shipping, and began an advertising campaign to entice other engine distributors to use our product, offering pricing that was very competitive. Within nine months, we had two distributors using our product, and we began expanding the product line to meet requests that were beginning to appear. In the second year of operation, we were remanufacturing not only engine components, but entire diesel engines, of all sizes. We were fortunate to have a young plant manager with a vision for innovation, and his expertise led us into totally new products. Within three years, we had several semitrailer trucks on the road delivering products to distributors in six states. The new company had grown from virtually nothing to over one hundred employees and $8 million in sales. This company was now carrying the combined companies financially. Initially it was thought to be suicidal to begin a second company with the financial burden we had. The collective wisdom of nearly everyone was to settle with the diesel engine company only—be safe, cut back more, and hope the interest rate would soon drop.

The growth of Bliss Enterprises wasn't without periods of crisis. Our company was located in an industrial park with several manufacturing companies, and we were the only nonunion organization in the group. This put a target on our back that created a lot of interest. In a three-year period, we were subjected to two union votes. Our company was a prime target, and the first vote caught us by surprise. After going through a lengthy pre-vote process, a union vote day was selected. On that day, my administrative assistant was provided an amount of money equal to one year's union dues and instructed to purchase as many groceries as possible. After bringing the groceries to the plant, we put them in our conference room with a sign over them indicating this represented one year of union dues. As employees came to work that day, we handed out raffle tickets to each, and the winner would receive all of the groceries. Needless to say, the union officials weren't too happy. The employees voted to remain nonunion.

A year and a half later, we faced a second union vote. The evening before the election, we decorated the entire plant with helium balloons and signs with the words "Congratulations to the winners" on them and had cake, soft drinks, and snacks on tables throughout the building. Again, the union officials weren't happy, but we told them we were celebrating the winners, whoever they may be! The employees voted again to remain nonunion.

> *Management Lesson: It's smart to seek advice—even smarter to listen to your "experts." However, if your instinct goes against the grain—and your confidence is strong— it may be smarter still to follow your vision.*

Top Three Tips

- Confidence is mandatory when you step into uncharted territory!

- Use new ideas!

- Hire intelligently!

Chapter Eleven
Another Call—Another Opportunity

"Whether you think you can or think you can't, you're right."
Henry Ford

After three growing years with Bliss Enterprises, I received an inquiry about the possibility of selling the company. Initially the idea was not appealing, as the remanufacturing company was highly profitable and, combined with the diesel engine company, made both companies an excellent combination. Selling the most profitable while retaining the marginal one wasn't particularly attractive. Relaying this to the potential buyer unexpectedly didn't negate the interest. It did, in fact, result in the interest of yet another potential buyer to purchase both companies.

Nearly a year was involved in putting together a package that was beneficial to all parties concerned, but it was finalized to the satisfaction of everyone. Then suddenly, for the first time in many years, I was faced without a company! But it didn't last very long.

"Failure seldom stops you. What stops you is the fear of failure."
Jack Lemmon

In starting a business, knowing your abilities—and your limitations—are important factors when determining the type of business you wish to acquire or start from scratch. The successful people shy away from areas where their expertise is limited and concentrate on their strengths. Having sold both companies, it was now necessary to decide which direction my life would take. Since it wouldn't be easy working for someone else, the answer came quickly—start another business. In analyzing my work history to date, it became clear that every position I had occupied was primarily one involving a new challenge. They were all problem-solving situations, many with no precedent to follow. Each had unique problems requiring different solutions. Using that as a springboard, the framework for a unique consulting company began to take shape.

R.L. Bliss & Associates, Inc., became a reality. This company would focus on assisting colleges, universities, and businesses having difficulties. In higher education, the areas of assistance would cover overall management, admissions, financial aid, development, and faculty/trustee relationships. For businesses, assistance was available in management, leadership, financial management, marketing and sales, and business plan preparation. In areas where my background was limited, such as financial accounting, contract professionals would be hired. A Web site was established outlining the services available, and within a few weeks inquiries began arriving. The intriguing part of the company was the background presented. Having served as both a college president and a corporate president was kind of unusual. There are, undoubtedly, many such individuals nationally, but it is not common to find that combination. This certainly aided in the initial attraction of the new company.

Top Three Tips

- Analyze your strengths.

- Determine your goals.

- Initiate your program.

Chapter Twelve
Another Company—A New Beginning

"If you aren't fired with enthusiasm,
you will be fired with enthusiasm."
Vince Lombardi

It's often said you can't be a hero in your own hometown, and initially this was proving true in the R.L. Bliss & Associates start-up company! Inquiries from the Web site were arriving on a regular basis, but all from states other than West Virginia. The majority were from colleges and universities seeking assistance in either admissions or development, but few were willing to pay for on-site visits. They were seeking help via the Internet—not exactly what we were looking for.

Management lesson: Experience is valuable, only if someone else desires your expertise. Patience and persistence are valuable allies.

A major breakthrough occurred when I was reading an article in the local newspaper that indicated Marshall University had hired a consultant from Idaho to review the Yeager Scholarship program. A letter was sent to the university president indicating my willingness to meet with him regarding this review. Since I had served as vice president of the nation's largest scholarship program (National Merit), the Yeager Scholarship program didn't appear to be a daunting task. Within a couple of weeks, the president responded, inviting me for a luncheon on the Marshall campus.

During this meeting, we discussed various segments of the university and where, if any, my background might be used. After a lengthy discussion, it was decided that my company would be placed on a monthly retainer to assist the president's office in a variety of areas, with the main emphasis on financial development. Marshall University became my first official client and, while on a month-to-month retainer, remained a client for the next four years.

Working with the vice president for development, we centralized the financial development into one office for more efficient control. Where previously each academic department, the athletic department, individual university organizations, and the development office were all contacting potential donors, the new office was organized to eliminate duplicate donor contacts, with all visits coordinated through the development office. This was a major change, and one made after considerable anguish in the athletic department.

While this was occurring, other clients began to appear. Private colleges in Illinois, Indiana, Texas, and Pennsylvania; state institutions in Michigan, Florida, and Texas; and finally numerous businesses in West Virginia became clients. In working with this variety of clients, a common thread began to appear in nearly every one.

Perception is an amazing word. It can be a positive or a negative, especially for the leader in either business or education. How one is perceived carries with it an anticipation of what is expected. Perception is usually defined as a selective cognitive process that lets a person make sense of stimuli from his/her environment. It entails the following three areas:

Self-concept: Self-image people hold
Self-esteem: How positively a person feels about his or her image
Self-presentation: Behavioral strategies used to affect how others see you

College and university presidents are perceived to be intelligent, have strong people skills, have the ability to work with multiple constituents, and be visionaries. Corporate and business presidents likewise are perceived to be intelligent, skilled at planning, financially astute, aggressive, and perhaps more inclined to be more stringent on performance. The perceptions held by employees in business and faculty in higher education of their presidents really will not vary a great deal. The one factor that permeates leaders in both areas is that of self-concept, the self-image they hold of themselves.

> *Management Lesson: Discovering how a president is perceived is not easy. Seeking accurate data is difficult—but it can be found in unusual places.*

Preparing for a campus visit involves a lot of time, reading and researching the background not only of the institution, but of the president as well. Remember my routine for campus visits while at National Merit? The same procedure was used many times with the new company. As stated earlier, students and faculty are very free with information when provided a free coke or coffee! Only by now I had learned to dress in blue jeans and a sweatshirt—not a shirt and tie. As before, my inquisition would also include local residents and, again, they were usually very forthcoming.

When the actual time arrived to meet with the university president, I felt I had a fairly good grasp on the institution. The initial meeting would begin with the usual get-acquainted conversation but would soon settle down to specific questions directed to the president. This is where the meeting would begin one of two possible scenarios. In the first scenario, presidents would view their performance as meeting the needs of nearly all of their constituents as best they could. Their self-perceptions would be that of a leader on top of everything, with their input mandatory in all decisions. It would not be uncommon for presidents like this to feel they were the most important individuals on the campus—they were the reason for the success to date (assuming this was the case). These presidents would be negligent in recognizing the importance of *people* as the major asset of the institution. And, usually, their perceptions of relations with students, faculty, and the local community would be far apart. When attempting to correct problems in specific areas of the university with these presidents, it would be extremely difficult to convince them that the underlying reason for the need for correction actually was in the president's office.

Up to this point in my career the four words of management (*people, communication, responsibility,* and *accountability*) had been instrumental in my business and education endeavors. It continually amazed me to find some leaders who would have strong convictions about accountability, but would place less stress on the importance of their people or the communication process. And they wondered why their leadership ability would be questioned.

The second scenario is one where presidents' views of their performance were matched fairly accurately with that received by students, faculty, and townspeople. These presidents realized the need for assistance in a particular area and wouldn't hesitate to initiate new procedures. This would usually begin with significant input from the current staff of the department under review, with input—where needed—from my staff and the president. Initiating change under this leadership is not threatening. It is, rather, exciting to everyone. The change, when implemented, is met with enthusiasm, and success is almost always a certainty.

Is perception a necessity to be analyzed? In my opinion, it is. A narrow self-perception can undermine and destroy a potential great leader.

Over the years, the opportunity was presented to work with several college and university presidents. Each was different; all had their own management style, some making a conscious effect to work cooperatively with their constituents in creating a better workplace and better institution. Others had other management styles, deciding they were the only ones capable of making decisions, only they could figure out the details of every decision in the institution. Without them the institution would undoubtedly not survive. It wasn't brain surgery to figure out why certain institutions were having difficulty. The difficulty was conveying to the leadership the true reason behind the weaknesses in the institution. Sometimes it worked—most often it didn't. There were some presidents who were so inept I couldn't help but wonder how they had attained their position! Thank goodness, the vast majority were truly great to work with and confirmed my belief that better results occur when you understand *people*, work with them, *communicate* regularly, give *responsibility* where and when necessary, and hold individuals *accountable* for the results.

> *"Few great men would have got past personnel."*
> *Paul Goodman*

Working with institutions of higher education was challenging on one hand and extremely satisfying on the other. The variety of personalities exceeded my expectations as did the wide variance in management styles. Business leaders, however, revealed a totally different breed of leadership. During my years as a corporate president and owner, I assumed my counterparts were astute in business and personnel matters. When business clients began to appear, my assumptions were proven wrong on far too many occasions!

During a period of four to five years, there were clients who were "successful" business presidents who "ruled" their companies through intimidation, fear, and retaliation. Employee turnover was high, and the presidents would fault the employees' "lack of devotion" to the company. Those who departed were said to be "not the best employee," yet strangely most managed to find employment in a similar organization and do very well. Clients of this type were continually amazed their company wasn't doing as well as it should—morale was usually relatively low, compensation was usually in the middle for comparable companies, fringe benefits were OK—not the highest—and not unexpectedly, production rarely managed to meet the expectations of management.

Working with individuals like this was a challenge. Some began to make needed changes, albeit reluctantly, when the economic benefits were demonstrated—at least on paper. When they actually began to appear on the bottom line of the financial statement, a true learning experience would usually occur. There were always some who steadfastly refused to change anything, and both their time and mine were wasted.

Like higher education, for every business that produced a challenge, there were those with whom it was a true pleasure to work. Presidents who not only accepted change but encouraged it throughout their organization were the most productive, innovative, and ultimately the most successful.

Top Three Tips

- Use prior experience to enhance a new opportunity.

- Be honest and constructive in suggesting changes.

- Accept the wide variance in management styles.

Chapter Thirteen
Unique Opportunities

"Don't tell people how to do things. Tell them what to do and let them surprise you with the results."
George S. Patton

Over a period of approximately ten years, there were three businesses/corporations and one educational institution where my full-time employment was required/requested. Each presented a situation requiring change—change in operation, change in personnel (in some cases), and a change in leadership. Following is a brief outline and description of each scenario, including the opportunities presented and the management challenges.

Mining Supply Company:

The young owner of this company had recently moved his residence to another state and was concerned about the management of his branch in West Virginia. He was expanding the company in other states, and his presence was required to finalize the start-up. We had an agreement that my tenure would not exceed one year or until the company was making a profit.

With my background in the diesel engine business, it wasn't difficult to grasp the mission of the company. Locating the customers was also not difficult, as many were the same customers of my former company. The main concern was the "change factor" in management—someone new coming on the scene, creating apprehension about jobs and futures. It became clear the immediate task would be to ease the change factor fear among employees. Individual meetings were held with employees to learn about them—their jobs, their backgrounds, their families, hobbies, and future goals. Since the majority of business was with mining companies, there were several salespersons covering every operating business. Schedules were designed to enable me to travel with each of the sales representatives for a minimum of one day, working with them and discussing their positions. We also started a company newsletter to keep employees up-to-date on activities and customer news. Walk-through sessions in the plant were held several times a day, seeking information on various orders and possible situations that might hold up orders. By the end of the first year, the company was doing well financially and internally. The time had arrived to get back to the consulting company.

Private Psychological Company:

It continually amazes me where business opportunities appear. Playing in a charity golf tournament, I happened to be paired with a PhD psychologist who owned his own company. During the course of the day, we agreed to meet in the next couple of weeks to discuss how we might work together. It didn't take long to determine this gentleman was extremely bright and was considered one of the best clinical psychologists in the state. At this time he had forty-two clinicians on staff and a strong client base. His problem wasn't a lack of either—it was a sincere desire to do everything possible for his staff. This included wages that exceeded the amount required to operate the business and meet monthly expenses.

The following month I became the general manager of the company with the charge to "do what is necessary to bring financial stability to the company." This presented a totally different approach, as it required a drastic change in operation. Individual meetings were held with each clinician, and expectations were discussed. Initially they had been hired as contract employees; however, in the ensuing years, this had slowly evolved into their being company employees. Their office material, supplies, and so forth were all furnished, as was office space. Additionally, each clinician was receiving a much higher percentage of the client fees than the company. The bottom line was the company was losing money while the clinicians were doing quite well.

The individual meetings were very direct in terms of longevity for the company if it continued at the present pace. The majority of clinicians were in agreement; however, there were others who steadfastly wouldn't discuss any changes in compensation. When weighing the existence of the company versus continuing business as usual, it became apparent within a few days that changes had to be made. Again, after I met individually with the staff, reductions in client fee percentages were initiated, and full application of clinicians serving as contract workers was established, including charges for office supplies, office space rental, and telephone use. Within sixty days, the professional staff dwindled from forty-two to twenty. Needless to say, my nickname became "Ax Man" in a very short time. Change had to be made for survival, and the company was at least on solid ground financially. This change drew the attention of another health-care organization, which led to yet another opportunity.

Management Lesson: To save a declining organization takes firm determination, ingenuity, compassion, and a

realization that you are going to be viewed by some as the
enemy—it is mandatory to leave your ego at the door.

Home Health-Care Facility:

The president of a local mental health facility contacted me nearing the close of my affiliation with the above company. He was interested in the possibility of perhaps merging his company with the now-reduced clinical practice. His facility was in need of additional clinicians, and a possible merger might work well for both entities. After several meetings, the details were complete, and the merger became official. During the process, the president indicated he had another operation, a home health-care company that was in need of new direction. We discussed the possibilities at length, and within another few weeks, I became the director of the largest home health-care facility in the state—again, entering into a professional field where I had very little knowledge or experience.

The first day on the job eyebrows were raised throughout the company when the new director was introduced—especially when my background was revealed. It was a certainty that many in attendance that day imagined my tenure would be brief and uneventful. The same comments were heard from employees: "He has no experience in home health!" Once again, the same four words (people, communication, responsibility, and accountability) began running through my brain as I set about to meet my new employees collectively and individually. As in the diesel engine company, it soon became apparent there were some department heads who were victims of "the Peter Principle"—having risen to the level of their incompetence. They were excellent practitioners, but they were placed in a management position due to their clinical knowledge, not their management knowledge or training. In individual meetings, nearly all acknowledged they would be much happier as a case worker and not as a department manager. With this information, the next task was to locate potential leaders among the current staff, and to my relief, there were several who ultimately would fill these positions. They understood the importance of working with people, not through or around them, and they left their egos at the door.

"Common sense is the knack of seeing things as they are,
and doing things as they ought to be done."
Josh Billings

Within the next few months, the company was running smoothly with the proper people in place. We had the "right people on the bus and in the right seats." Service was exceptional, and the "new boss" was accepted into this new venture. The highlight came several months after my departure in a letter from one of the nurses.

> *Bob, Just a note to thank you for showing me what true organizational leadership is all about. Believe it or not, I watched in awe that a man with no health care experience could run a home health agency. I understand now and can appreciate the example you set. Your leadership style helped develop me into the kind of leader I am proud to be. Thank you from the bottom of my heart.*

> *Management lesson: Experience has taught me that people are basically willing and eager to accept leadership outside of their profession—provided the new leader exhibits the same willingness and eagerness to learn.*

After two years, the home health agency was running fine, and the inevitable happened yet again—a telephone call. A friend of my wife called, indicating the company she was with had just lost its president and she had submitted my name for consideration. She told me to be prepared for a telephone call from them in the very near future.

For-Profit Education Company:

Sure enough, about two weeks later, the call arrived, and I was invited to meet with an official of the parent company. Fortunately, this company was located rather close to my hometown, so travel wasn't a consideration. Meeting with the regional vice president took place soon after, and following three hours of discussion, it was agreed I should fly to the parent headquarters in California to interview with the corporate executives.

Once again, I was about to venture into education, but this time it would be education with a slightly different twist. The parent company was one of the largest for-profit education companies in the nation. At this point, it had approximately 190 institutions under its umbrella. The institution at my location was not a degree-granting school; it was specializing in vocational programs such as massage therapy, electronics, nurse's aides, pharmacy technician, homeland security, and medical specialists. Enrollment normally would be around five hundred students. It was going to be a totally different perspective of education, and one that would add further to my overall knowledge of management.

The trip to California was enlightening to say the least. The vice president was very astute, intelligent, and engaging—very likeable. We spent the day discussing the financial situation at "my" school as well as the possibilities for expansion. He expressed some concern about my lack of experience in the for-profit world, but I countered that by enlightening him to the fact that every position on my resume had been one of for-profit, including the traditional colleges and universities. While designated as nonprofit, it was still necessary that they meet a budget and operate prudently while exercising sound financial measures. Throughout the day, I had interviews with various other executives, concluding with a final meeting with the initial vice president. He indicated he would be in touch within the next ten days.

My wife and I had scheduled a vacation to see friends in Florida immediately upon my return from California. I was on the golf course when my cell phone rang. It was California calling, and the position of president was mine. This was on Thursday, and they wanted me on the job the following Monday. We finally settled on the following Tuesday to report for work.

"The smart ones ask when they don't know.
And, sometimes when they do."
Malcolm Forbes

Walking into yet another totally foreign situation is always exhilarating and somewhat frightening as well. It's exciting to uncover the challenges and yet frightening to discover just how many there are! In conversations with the corporate executives, I was informed the school had gone through three presidents in a rather short period. There were several employees with long tenures who were pretty well locked into their routine, and change was not to their liking. Again—facing the challenge of a new face in an established, ongoing company—lots of fun!

In the first week, all of the department heads and faculty members were interviewed individually. Morale was pretty good, but the usual apprehension was present about yet another management change and how it would impact each of them. When they were reassured their positions were not in jeopardy (at that time), they were very candid in their appraisals of their jobs and the school in total. Learning the basics of the courses offered took some time, but by visiting classrooms and talking with students, I quickly absorbed it. Asking questions became routine, and the more questions I asked, the more comfortable the employees became—and they were becoming more open to change. Most of the change would come from their suggestions, and this added to the new feeling of importance among them.

Completely unexpected was the desire for complete oversight by the parent company in California on the day-to-day operation of the school. Initially they indicated they wanted expansion—new programs and perhaps even a new building to accommodate a larger enrollment. After I called upon previous contacts, it became apparent there were several possible areas for program expansion. But initiating new programs would definitely require more space, if not an entirely new facility. Plans were established outlining a business plan for both new programs and expansion. Internal meetings were held, and the faculty became excited about the possibilities. Their input in the planning was invaluable. When the plans were discussed with corporate officers, they kept putting off an answer giving the go-ahead for additional planning. As time went by, this became an irritant to everyone, and in a short time, I realized that expansion probably would not happen. Another aspect of the company was advertising. All advertising was controlled and designed in California without regard to local wants or needs. I learned many years earlier that advertising of any kind must be geared to the clientele you are planning to serve—and advertising featuring blond, sun-baked students in well-lighted, well-equipped classrooms didn't fit the norm for West Virginia. The results indicated as much, but not enough to convince the folks in California.

After two years, this school was called one of the "jewels" of the company for profitability, morale among faculty, and a progressive outlook for the future. However, it was apparent the control strings were not in the school, and they were becoming even less so. Micromanaging has never been one of my strong suits. I don't believe in handling employees in that manner and have a difficult time being micromanaged myself.

"A leader is best when people barely know he exists.
When his work is done, his aim fulfilled, they will say,
'We did it ourselves.'"
Lao-Tzu

While working at the school, I wanted to keep my hand in higher education as well, so for roughly three years I taught management classes for Wheeling Jesuit University. They offered a master's program in Charleston, and my class was offered every Thursday evening. This experience proved—once again—to be useful very soon in an upcoming conversation.

"Life appears to me too short to be spent in nursing
animosity or registering wrongs."
Charlotte Bronte

Conditions at the for-profit school became very routine and very much controlled beyond the boundary of West Virginia. Even the regional vice president acknowledged the seemingly high degree of centralized management, while not quite totally ignoring local management. About this time, an article appeared in the local newspaper indicating the director of the Executive MBA program at the University of Charleston was possibly leaving. In expecting to teach a course in that program,

I made a telephone call to the university president. He asked that I come to the university and meet with the provost, the chair of the Business Division, and the director of the Executive MBA (EMBA) program to determine what course or courses might be applicable for my participation. This would lead to a nearly complete circle in my professional career. The discussion would be totally different from my expectations. Once again, a challenge would be presented.

"When you're through changing, you're through."
Bruce Barton

Top Three Tips

- Regardless of the occupation, most employees will respond to a leader who cares.

- Micromanaging is not good for an entrepreneur.

- Keeping abreast of change in other occupations is always good.

Chapter Fourteen
Returning to a University Campus

*"The trouble with learning from experience
is that you never graduate."*
Doug Larson

On the agreed-upon day and time, I arrived on the campus of the University of Charleston. As I was on the way up the outside stairs, the president was coming down and remarked, "The provost is waiting for you in his office." Going down the main hallway, I went into the office and was introduced to the provost, Dr. Charles Stebbins. Every once in awhile you meet someone with whom an immediate connection is made—you like the person from the initial handshake. Such was the case with Dr. Stebbins. A retired air force general, he had been on the job of provost for about a week! After making introductory comments for a few moments, I inquired if the chair of the Business Division was going to join us. Dr. Stebbins replied he wasn't—he had resigned a few days ago. When asked about the director of the EMBA program, he replied that he, too, had resigned. My mind immediately began wondering, "Then why am I here?"

The question was quickly answered. The provost inquired if I would have an interest in returning to the university as the chair of the Business Division and director of the EMBA program. At this point, a slight breeze would have knocked me off my chair. This question came completely out of the blue and, quite naturally, caught me totally by surprise. The Business Division had been going through a succession of leaders recently, and the EMBA program was literally dying on the vine at this time. In previous years, the EMBA had flourished, and the one program offered annually would be full. The reason or reasons for the decline weren't immediately known, but the reality was the program would require a significant operational change in a short period of time. In the next several minutes, Charlie and I (we were now on a first name basis!) discussed the pluses and minuses of the position, including the personnel currently in the Business Division. The meeting adjourned without an answer, but with a lot of questions.

One week later—once again while I was on the golf course, but with the regional vice president of the for-profit company where I was still employed—a telephone call was received from Dr. Stebbins, and I informed him the offer was accepted. That was followed by a meeting in the golf cart with the regional vice president to notify him of my decision. He understood, and we parted on a friendly basis. Five days later, my latest challenge waited as I walked once again up the stairs to the University of Charleston.

After I briefly met with the provost, he led me to the Business Division office complex on the third floor. There I was introduced to two faculty members who just happened to be the most tenured in service, having worked there thirty-one years and twenty-five years, respectively. Their eyes told the story I had seen many times before— here's another new guy, how long will he last, what will he try to do? Their questions were valid, and once again, meetings were held quickly with all faculty members to introduce myself and to learn more about them, collectively and individually. Once again, the challenges quickly surfaced—not enough faculty members, rapid turnover in management, declining enrollment in the EMBA program, and lack of instructors in the EMBA program. The EMBA program was not where the president wanted it, either academically or in numbers. The former director was conducting one program yearly, and the one I would inherit had only eleven candidates.

My favorite words took on meaning—*people:* there was an immediate need for at least one new faculty member to meet the growing business major enrollment; *communication:* there was an immediate need to keep faculty informed on the many changes to be made; *responsibility:* there was a need to tap into the resources available within the faculty for specific projects; and *accountability:* there was a need to reward those who not only accepted the responsibility but actually relished the accountability aspect. With that in mind, a meeting of all Business Division faculty was scheduled. During the meeting, my background was introduced, my basic management philosophy was discussed, and then each faculty member was asked to give a brief statement on their background, their concerns, and their ambitions within their area of academic responsibility. Then it was time to begin with changes.

> *"Nothing happens… but first a dream."*
> *Carl Sandburg*

The Executive MBA program would be my first challenge. The program was scheduled to begin a new class the Friday after I reported on campus. The curriculum needed change. MBA enrollments nationally had been dropping for the previous five years. The drop wasn't due to lack of interest in the degree, but rather in the content being taught. Colleges and universities across the country were having their MBA classes taught by very bright professors, but a high percentage were recent recipients of doctorate degrees who were trained, not in business, but in research.

They entered the MBA classroom and proceeded to give instruction in research methods—not necessarily business-oriented, problem-based instruction. Also, a large number of professors had never had to meet a payroll themselves, let alone own be responsible for a business. They taught largely from textbooks, and the credibility of many instructors was questioned due to this lack of business experience. The result was a decline in MBA candidates. Businesses wanted graduates who could think creatively, be innovative in business, solve problems, and make intelligent decisions to prevent recurrences. With that in mind, and in the four days before teaching my first class, our curriculum was revamped to be aimed at graduating candidates who would be ready to not only meet the expectations of employers, but be prepared to move rapidly up the management ladder.

Two of the senior faculty members on my staff were immediately tagged to once again teach in this program. Both had taught previously, but for reasons unknown to me, they were dropped from the program before my arrival. One had thirty-plus years of experience, academically and in business. The other had twenty-five years' experience, including serving as the president of a multinational holding company. This was experience that *had* to be used in the classroom, and they were promptly returned to the MBA faculty. In addition to the faculty, the original intent was to bring local, state, and national business leaders in occasionally to speak to the class. In the preceding two or three years, they had brought in two or three speakers per program. This number was immediately increased to a minimum of thirty-five speakers in every program and would sometimes range as high as fifty speakers. The list included U.S. representatives, corporation presidents, bank presidents, presidents of various national accounting firms, state government officials, city government officials, and health-care executives. Instructors, all having experience in business, did not dwell on philosophy, but did use practical business experiences and problem solving. The foundational philosophy of business is important, and the students are required to read selected textbooks on the topic, but the prime emphasis is on practical-based learning. To maintain my student and faculty contact, , I taught (and continue to teach) the first module of each program. There are five modules, each with a different instructor and each with a specific learning outcome. The message we sent loud and clear was that we train leaders—future CEOs—and they graduate prepared to meet that challenge.

The result of our efforts has exceeded expectations. Beginning with one class of eleven candidates and only two corporations sending employees to us for the program, three years later we now have three programs operating simultaneously with a maximum enrollment of twenty in each, and sixty-four corporations are now sending employees to our program. This could not have been accomplished without the people in the Business Division buying in to the new format, bringing their expertise and enthusiasm into the classroom, and communicating their belief in the change.

While this was going on, attention was also given to the undergraduate program of the division. The faculty had experienced several changes in leadership in the previous months and, despite our earlier meeting, still had reservations about the "new guy" in charge. Micromanaging is not my style. Never has been and hopefully never will be. From experience, I learned that I could not be micromanaged, and that has played a major part in my management style. The faculty were assured they would not be micromanaged. They were all professionals and would be treated as such, unless they gave me a reason to believe otherwise. Treating people in this manner does a number of things. First, it enables them to make decisions—and to make mistakes. This usually makes them think longer before making a decision, requiring a more thorough thought process. Second, it helps them learn, should mistakes occur. Few intelligent people will make the same mistake multiple times—and if they do, that's when intervention is required by management. Third, it gives the individual a feeling of importance in the overall program. They give the best contribution they can and sometimes are embarrassed when they do make mistakes. Fourth, it saves time! When employees are empowered within their area of responsibility to make decisions, everything moves faster. I call this simply "the lazy man's philosophy of management." Give the employee an area of responsibility, outline together the expectations and the time requirements (if any), then get out of the way and let them do their work. Reward the top performers, and work with those who may fall below expectations. Terminations are not pleasant when job expectations aren't accomplished; however, termination is probably not the employee's fault entirely. Maybe you hired wrong, maybe you didn't train properly, or maybe you failed to provide the tools to succeed. All of this was brought to the table with the Business Division faculty. To date, they have responded extremely well. Have we lost faculty? Sure, it's not uncommon to have good employees depart for higher positions, but it's a compliment to the university and our hiring practices when this occurs.

"The best sermons are lived, not preached."
Cowboy wisdom

Once the undergraduate programs and the Executive MBA programs were moving forward, it was time to look at expansion into new programs and to put into place some of the philosophies the faculty and staff had been listening to. Over a period of eighteen months, two individuals had brought two separate ideas for new programs to my attention. It would have been easy to brush them off and continue with our existing programs, but the excitement of adding totally new programs was enticing.

> *Management Lesson: Sometimes the best ideas come from those outside the normal workplace. Listening and sharing ideas may lead to a far superior program than you could have imagined by yourself.* **Be sure to recognize those who brought the program to life initially!** *Don't take credit for yourself.*

The first program was a proposed master's degree in forensic accounting (MFA) and was brought to my attention by Dr. Robert Rufus. Dr. Rufus not only headed his own accounting firm, but for the previous fifteen years had been heavily involved in the field of forensic accounting. Having no prior knowledge of this field, my conversations with him quickly convinced me this was an opportunity that should be explored. During the next eighteen months, an executive master of forensic accounting program was designed, syllabus created, and national accreditation received. The first program began in January 2009. It became the nation's first Executive MFA program and quickly gained widespread interest. Hiring the state's leading forensic accountants and lawyers, the program began with the intent of eventually surpassing the Executive MBA in popularity and in numbers.

The second program was suggested by Wake Buxton, senior vice president and director of Advance Planning at a local Charleston bank. The two of us discussed the possibility of creating the first certified financial planner (CFP) program in West Virginia. Surrounding states were conducting several such programs, and individuals within West Virginia wishing to pursue this program had no option other than traveling out of state. Again, after working together for several months, Mr. Buxton put together the curriculum and began looking for highly qualified faculty. At the same time, he applied to attain full accreditation from the National Certified Planner Board of Standards, Inc. As with the previous program, the CFP program began in January 2009, with candidates arriving from all over West Virginia as well as Pennsylvania.

Opportunities are found virtually everywhere, but you have to be persistent in seeking them out. The fun part of creating new programs is the puzzle of determining the ones that will be successful.

"Nothing in the world can take the place of persistence. Talent will not; nothing is more common than unsuccessful men with talent. Genius will not; unrewarded genius is almost a proverb. Education will not; the world is full of educated failures. Persistence and determination alone are omnipotent."
Calvin Coolidge

Top Three Tips

- Always prioritize your challenges.

- Seek others' advice in creating new ventures.

- Be persistent in reaching specified goals.

Chapter Fifteen
Future Challenges Exist Somewhere

"We don't know one millionth of one percent about anything."
Thomas Edison

The University of Charleston has been exciting, frustrating, and educational for the past three-plus years. Returning to a college campus again after many years in business has been a terrific experience. The friendships made, the feeling of giving of oneself to up-and-coming business leaders, and the satisfaction of having made a contribution to the business community is a wonderful feeling. Like my work with the National Merit Scholarship Corporation, right now the University of Charleston could very well be my last employer—*or* that darn telephone may someday ring, and with it will come yet another challenge that just very well could be one that is too tempting to refuse.

"Twenty years from now you will be more disappointed
by the things you didn't do, than by the ones you did do.
So throw off the bowlines. Sail away from the safe harbor.
Catch the trade winds in your sails.
Explore - Dream - Discover."
Mark Twain

Top Three Tips

- The challenges never sought are the ones that usually appear.

- Satisfaction with oneself is healthy and comfortable.

- Always be prepared for the unexpected.

Epilogue

Since early childhood, my life has rarely followed a predetermined path. It's been an adventure few experience—combining management in higher education and business. The challenges have been many, and some appeared overwhelming at times. But like any challenges, they became less frightening as they were placed in context. None were life threatening, and while they very well could have become "job threatening," fortunately, this never occurred. As in any position of leadership, there were times when decisions regarding possible upward changes were required. In the majority of my situations it would have been easy to remain in the current position at that time—and to be happy. But somewhere in the part of the mind I'm not qualified to dissect, a feeling of seeking challenges was always present—and still is to this day.

Is there "one way" to manage people? Absolutely not, but there are similarities that seem to be present in the success of nearly all good leaders—in business and in higher education. Attempting to follow or imitate the management style of one person is certain to lead to disarray. Rarely are two individuals exactly alike, in personality, temperament, or management. Finding the right combination is delicate and continually changing as situations change. The successful leader will realize this and will adapt to the needs of the organization. Too many times executives view themselves as the "savior" when arriving in a new position—nothing could be further from the truth. They are, in fact, perhaps the least informed at that point. It's always better to listen initially—to current employees, to former employees, and to customers. Form your plan—but never forget the basic four words that should play a major role in your career, and in your management of employees: People, communication, responsibility, and accountability.

Leadership is not an exact science. It takes time, experience, and an understanding of your own capabilities in management. Judging yourself is never easy, and frequently it isn't accurate. So are you the captain of the Love Boat? Are you constantly striving to please everyone and be liked? Or are you the captain of the Titanic? A good leader, but not prepared for the unexpected crisis situations? Are you prepared for managing effectively in times of turmoil and change? Only you can answer that, but you have to be true to yourself in doing so. Another great Clint Eastwood quote, "A man's got to know his limitations," is very accurate, especially when you're confronted with difficult situations in management. Knowing when and how to steer your company through a storm is a management necessity, because that day will come—and possibly quicker than you realize. The Boy Scout motto, "Be prepared," is one to remember as you rise in management ranks and, most definitely, should already be in place for current presidents and CEOs. The current business climate demands no less.

I've been fortunate, having the opportunity to observe and learn from some of the top CEOs in the nation, in business and higher education. In every scenario I have taken away significant knowledge in management and leadership—some good and some not so good. But in each case, there were events that added to my management style. People change—and your management style should change accordingly. Hopefully, you will have the same opportunities of experiencing a wide variety of leaders in a broad spectrum of management situations. If so, learn from them—bring the positive changes into your style, and discard the ones that no longer apply. It takes courage to change, to adapt, and to innovate, but your ship will always sail smoothly, and you will find yourself capable of managing in a much wider range of professions. Trust me—it works!

"Courage does not always roar. Sometimes it is a quiet voice at the end of the day, saying, "I will try again tomorrow."
Mary Anne Radmacher

Biography of Robert L. Bliss

 A native of Adrian, Michigan, and now residing in Charleston, West Virginia, Bob Bliss has had an exciting and distinguished career in higher education and business. He has been president and/or owner of four corporations and held responsible positions, including president, in four institutions of higher education. Starting with a consulting arrangement, he has also served in leadership positions for an additional four companies.

With one management degree from Michigan State University and two degrees from Adrian College, his unique background has enabled him to work effectively with both businesses and education institutions nationally. His expertise encompasses nearly all areas of management, and he has a record of effectively reversing financial difficulties in business and management concerns in higher education.

In demand as a public speaker, he is an avid golfer, reader, and a pilot, holding instrument, multiengine, and commercial pilot ratings.

Bob Bliss may be contacted at:
rbliss@suddenlink.net or www.bobblissspeaks.com

Printed in the United States
144451LV00003B/3/P